Giant African
Land Snails
for Beginners

ALINA DARIA

Contents

Family, Genera and Species

Achatinoidea? Achatinidae? Archachatina? Achatina? Aren't they all the same? What is the difference? And who is supposed to be able to remember - let alone pronounce - that anyway? You have to admit: For a layperson, all these designations are confusing at first. But once you have understood the classifications, things look very different!

African giant snails are a family of specific snails and the scientific name of this family is 'Achatinidae'. The family Achatinidae was identified in 1840 by the British William Swainson (1789-1855), who worked as a malacologist, among other things. Malacologists study molluscs, which also include snails.

In zoology, there is often a superfamily ('superfamilia') and/or subfamilies ('subfamilia') in addition to the family. The family of Achatinidae - the African giant snails - also belongs to a superfamily. The superfamily is the 'Achatinoidea'.

Animals are not only assigned to families, but also to orders. The orders are placed above the families. African giant snails belong to the order of the lung snails and within this to the more specific suborder of the lung snails.

However, there is not only the subfamily Achatinidae, which goes back to William Swainson, but several other subfamilies - for example, the subfamily Coeliaxinae or the Petriolinae. However, we focus on the Achatinidae subfamily, as the best-known and most popular species belong to this family.

So far, so good. So, the Achatinidae is a family in the animal kingdom - and this is what we want to deal with in more detail in this book. But this is not the end, because the families are further broken down into genera and then into species.

The genera are one rank below the families in the hierarchy. Usually, several species belong to one genus. However, it is also possible that only one species belongs to a genus - in which case the genus is called 'monotypic'.

Each species has a two-part scientific name. The first part of the name is the genus to which the species belongs, and the second part of the name is the species epithet. An epithet is simply an addition.

There are many genera in the African Giant Snail family - fourteen of them - and these genera include many different species. As it would go beyond the scope of this book to consider all these species, we will concentrate on the two best-known and most popular genera: the genus 'Achatina' and the genus

'Archachatina'. However, the genus 'Lissachatina', for example, is also very popular in the home terrarium!

However, it should also be mentioned that strictly speaking 'Lissachatina' was a subgenus of 'Achatina'. But in the course of time it was found that the differences between Achatina and Lissachatina are so great that it is justified and necessary to no longer keep Lissachatina as a subgenus, but as a genus of its own - hence Lissachatina was elevated to an 'independent' genus.

The different genera of African Giant Snails differ in shape, colour and size of both the soft bodies and the shells of the snails.

The greatest differences between the two genera 'Achatina' and 'Archachatina' lie in ...

... the columella - this is the spindle of the snail shell, which runs from the mouth of the shell to the apex and whose circumferences touch each other;

... the end of the apex - this is the tip of the snail shell;

... and the size of the eggs.

Snails belonging to the Achatina genus lay very small eggs in a very high number. Usually, the eggs are only about five millimetres in size. Sometimes the eggs reach a size of eight millimetres, which is still quite small. However, about three hundred eggs are laid.

But it must be mentioned that there are also three Achatina species that are viviparous! These exceptions are the species Achatina craveni, Achatina zanzibarica and Achatina allisa.

The eggs of the snails that belong to the Archachatina genus are considerably larger at about two centimetres. The apex of the Archachatina snails is also rounded, while the apex of the Achatina species is pointed!

The genera then include the various species on the next level. Probably the most popular species of the Achatina genus is Achatina achatina.

Well-known species belonging to the genus Archachatina are, for example, Archachatina marginata ovum, Archachatina marginata suturalis or Archachatina rhodostoma.

The popular Lissachatina species include Lissachatina fulica, Lissachatina allisa or Lissachatina reticulata.

Fun Fact: Snails belonging to different genera usually cannot mate with each other! An Achatina snail, for example, will usually not be able to mate with an Archachatina snail. With the individual species belonging to the same genus, however, the situation is quite different! Here, mating is normally possible.

In theory, for example, an Archachatina rhodostoma can mate with an Archachatina marginata ovum. Such a mating would result in a hybrid. In practice, however, this is almost never done, because on the one hand it does not contribute to the clear conservation of the species and on the other hand it is not good for the snails in many cases, because sometimes the species have different needs, which then mix.

© Ell Wi

Origin and Life in the Wild

Since the family of Achatinidae is called Giant African land snails, the origin of these snails can already be deduced from this. Nowadays, those snails can be found as pets on all continents, but their home is on the African continent, and they live there in the wild.

Giant African land snails, i.e., snails from the family Achatinidae, are found south of the Sahara desert. The distribution area begins approximately at the level of Senegal. Senegal is a country in the far west of Africa, which lies below Mauritania and borders the sea in the west. From here, the range of giant African land snails extends across the entire continent to Somalia, which lies in the easternmost part of Africa and also borders the sea. From this altitude, the range extends across the rest of the continent - all the way to South Africa in the far south. However, most of the different species are found in Central Africa.

As a rule, most giant African land snails live in tropical rainforests. Most species prefer a humid climate, as it prevails in the tropics. However, there are also species that live in savannahs, where it is drier than in the rainforest. A few smaller species can also be found in deserts, but this is rather rare. In principle, it can be said that the majority of giant African land snails prefer and need humid areas.

The majority of giant African land snails are dependent on such a climate, as otherwise desiccation can be imminent. This is also the reason why most giant African land snails are nocturnal. Since they are so sensitive to dryness, it is a good idea for them to rest during the day and only become active towards dusk. However, many snails are also capable of closing their shells when dryness threatens. Nevertheless, this danger should be minimised.

Although giant African land snails have their home in Africa and are most commonly found there, some species have also been "introduced" to other countries and islands. Therefore, they are no longer found exclusively in Africa. The species that has probably spread the most is Lissachatina fulica.

© *Barbara Konwischer*

Physiology

Snails belong to the phylum Mollusca (molluscs), more precisely to the subphylum Conchifera (shell molluscs), which do not have a skeleton. The body of molluscs consists only of the head, foot, viscera and sometimes a shell as in giant African land snails.

The scientific name of all snails is 'Gastropoda', which is derived from the Greek and means 'abdominal animal'. This name alludes to the foot, which is located on the ventral side of the snail and is used for locomotion. The foot is very muscular and swellable. The snail moves by alternately contracting and tensing the individual muscles within the foot ("contraction"). Essential here are the transverse and longitudinal muscles located on the sole of the foot.

However, snails are the only molluscs that (also) live on land. Other molluscs include mussels and squid.

The head of a snail is quite different from the heads of mammals, reptiles, etc. The head is not clearly separated from the foot - i.e., from the creeping muscle - but they merge smoothly. Some people assume that snails do not have eyes, but this is not correct - the eyes of giant African land snails are located at the end of the two long antennae and are not necessarily clearly recognisable as eyes to a layperson, because they simply look like black dots on the antennae. The eyes are also not particularly well developed, and the giant African land snail cannot see far with them. The field of vision extends to only a few centimetres.

The mouth of giant African land snails is also quite special, as they do not have classic teeth. To grind their food, giant African land snails use their tongue, which is called a "radula". This term comes from Latin and means something like "to rasp". With the help of this rasping tongue, the snail can rasp and grind the food.

There are regularly arranged rows of tiny "chitin teeth" on the radula. Strictly speaking, the radula is not a classical tongue, but a tongue-like lamella that sits in the radula pocket.

As we already know, giant African land snails live mainly in areas with very high humidity, for example in tropical rainforests. There, a humidity of 90% is normal. Giant African land snails cannot cope with a climate that is too dry and may have to take a so-called dry rest, which can sometimes last up to several months. During dry dormancy, the giant African land snail buries itself in the substrate and seals its shell with a layer of lime and slime, which, however, allows air to pass through. If the humidity rises, the snail can break open this layer and behave normally again.

Giant African land snails have a special shell shape that distinguishes them, for example, from European snails such as the very well-known Roman snail. The shell of giant African land snails also varies from species to species in terms of shape, size and colour, but the shells of giant African land snails are always quite narrow, and they taper to a cone shape. The apex - i.e., the tip of the shell - is pointed in almost all species and is directed backwards (not to the side as in the Roman snail).

In snails, the shell spindle that connects the spindle muscle to the soft snail body is called the columella. The columella can be easily seen if you look at the giant African land snail from below. What the columella looks like, however, varies quite a bit from species to species, as it can be reddish or whitish or even purple, for example.

The breathing hole of the snails is also called the "mantle opening". The mantle partially encloses the visceral sac and releases lime into the shell to keep it stable and to make minor repairs. There is the breathing hole, which can be opened and completely closed with the help of muscles.

Giant African land snails have their genitals on the head. The genital openings are located next to the right eye sensor. Here the giant African land snail has both its penis and its vagina. When mating, both snails insert their penis into the respective opening of the other snail.

But not only the genitals are in a different place than in most other animals and humans. The anus is also in a rather unusual place, as it is found at the front of the mantle cavity.

Besides the head, the crawling foot, the shell and the mantle, snails also have a visceral sac. As the name suggests, this sac contains the snail's internal organs. The visceral sac is partially enclosed by the mantle.

Unlike most animals, the giant African land snail does not breathe through its mouth. The mouth opening is only used by the snail to taste and pick up or rasp food; respiration takes place in a different way.

On the one hand, the giant African land snail breathes actively through muscle movements, because muscle contraction causes fresh air to flow into the lungs from the outside, as the floor in the respiratory cavity is flattened with the help of this muscle contraction so that air can flow in. The lung is a network of vessels in the mantle cavity. Unlike some other snails, giant African land snails do not breathe by means of gills or trachea.

The air can enter the snail's lungs, which carry the fresh oxygen through the body and primarily to the heart. On the other hand, however, the giant African land snail can also breathe through the skin. However, skin breathing is not the primary method of breathing, but an additional one.

And what about the other organs? Which bodily functions does the giant African land snail still have and which ones does it lack? What senses does it have to fall back on?

Senses:

1. Smelling: Giant African land snails do not have a nose but smell by means of their antennae. They have two long and two shorter antennae on their head. The long antennae, which are located above the short ones, each house an eye, but also sensory cells for smelling and touching. The lower, shorter antennae are also equipped with olfactory sensory cells, but with fewer sensory cells than the upper antennae. Furthermore, there are also more olfactory sensory cells in the skin in the anterior mantle area and in the mouth area. Through the sense of smell, giant African land snails are able to seek out food or avoid pollutants and toxins as much as possible.

2. Taste: Giant African land snails can taste. They use their sense of taste to recognise their food, using the taste cells in the mouth opening and (to a lesser extent) also in the foot. They can perceive sour, salty, bitter and sweet tastes and often prefer sweet things (fruits or sweet vegetables). Bitter flavours are rather

avoided by many giant African land snails, although the rather bitter dandelion, for example, is also quite popular. The mouth opening is in fact only designed for tasting and ingesting food, as no respiration takes place here.

3. Touch/feel: Giant African land snails have a very fine and well-developed sense of touch, with which they can perceive vibrations and shocks very well, for example. This ability at least partially replaces the sense of hearing. The tactile organs are located in the skin of the giant African land snail - especially in the sole seam and in the antennae, there are particularly many and well-developed tactile cells.

4. Seeing: Giant African land snails can see, but this sense is rather poorly developed compared to the sense of touch, smell and taste. While humans are heavily dependent on their eyes, giant African land snails do use their eyes, but rely more heavily on the aforementioned three senses. The eyes of the giant African land snail are black, dotted eyes that sit on top

of the longer two antennae. However, giant African land snails cannot see very far with their eyes; presumably, the ability to see only extends to a few centimetres. However, giant African land snails also have light-sensing cells in their skin. These light-sensing cells cause the so-called shadow reflex, which usually causes the giant African land snail to retreat.

5. Hearing: Giant African land snails cannot hear, because acoustic sensory organs to perceive sound and tone are not present in any mollusc. Although giant African land snails do not perceive sound waves, they can of course feel vibrations - mainly because their sense of touch is very well developed and can sometimes replace the sense of hearing quite well.

In addition, giant African land snails have a so-called "sense of place" or "sense of position". They can find certain places they have already been to from quite a distance. How they manage to do this has not yet been conclusively and precisely explained. What is already generally known, however, is the fact that snails have so-called statocysts in their foot. These are the organs of equilibrium of snails and other invertebrates. They consist of a bladder that is filled with liquid and in which so-called statoliths are found. Statoliths are small grains of lime or sand. These bubbles react to the earth's gravity by touching these grains.

Other organs besides those already explained:

1. Heart: The heart of the giant African land snail consists of an antechamber and a ventricle. The function of the heart is the same as in humans - it pumps blood through the body and supplies oxygen to every part of the body. The pulmonary vein, which carries oxygen-rich blood to the heart, opens into the atrioventricular chamber; from here the blood is pumped on via the aorta. The heart of the giant African land snail pulsates rhythmically, but it beats faster in warm temperatures than in cold ones.

2. Liver: The liver is primarily a detoxification organ. Like the salivary glands, it secretes digestive juices and also stores fat reserves for times of need, such as times of drought or for the winter.

3. "Brain": The "brain" of the giant African land snail controls reflexes and movements, just as it does in humans. However, it is important to mention that, strictly speaking, snails do not have a classic brain. Instead, they have so-called "ganglia", which form the snails' sensory centre. These ganglia are nerve nodes or a cluster of nerve cell bodies that are highly concentrated and replace a classical brain, so to speak. The ganglia are distributed throughout the body but are particularly concentrated in the area of the antennae and also in the mouth area.

4. Kidney: The kidney is a detoxification organ that excretes whitish waste products. Unlike humans and most other animals, however, the snail has only one kidney (instead of two). The kidney is located in the visceral sac above the heart.

In addition, the shell is essential for the survival and protection of the snail. The snail shell is a kind of outer skeleton that protects the animal from dangers such as injuries, enemies or even dehydration. Minor injuries to the snail shell can often be repaired quite easily - often by the snail itself or with the help of human assistance. Larger injuries to the shell, however, often mean the death sentence for the snail, so good care should always be taken to protect the shell. Since the shell is made almost entirely of lime, a sufficient supply is immensely important - also to be able to carry out minor repairs and touch-ups. This "lime house" is covered with a fine layer of conchiolin. Conchiolin is a complex protein that protects the shell against acid.

But snails are probably best known for their mucus, which is often perceived as disgusting by humans, but is very important for the snails. Giant African land snails tend to produce rather little slime compared to many other snails, but they too depend on their slime. The mucus is secreted from the snails' skin glands and protects the animal from dehydration, for example, and surrounds the snail's body with a kind of water envelope. The snail's skin can absorb water from this shell. In this way, the snail covers about half of its water requirements. The mucus is also important for locomotion because it serves as a kind of "glide path" over which the snail can crawl. This glide path of mucus facilitates crawling for locomotion and also protects the sole of the crawling foot. In addition, the mucus makes it easier for the snail to adhere to different surfaces and also to crawl quite safely on upward or downward slopes.

© Shabalovich

Gender and Reproduction

People are used to dividing their pets into "males" and "females". But giant African land snails are also very special companions in this respect! They are in fact hermaphrodites. Hermaphroditic animals are both male and female, and they have both reproductive organs.

The term comes from the Greek and is a word combination of "Hermes" and "Aphrodite". Hermes is a Greek god, while Aphrodite is a Greek goddess - that is, a man and a woman.

The term 'hermaphrodite' is now derived from the name of the Greek figure 'Hermaphroditos'. Hermaphroditos is sometimes worshipped as a deity in Greek mythology - especially in Cyprus - but not consistently regarded as a deity. Hermaphroditos exhibits both female and male bodily characteristics, which are said to have been acquired through a fusion with a nymph. Hermaphroditos is not the only hermaphrodite in Greek mythology, but it is the best known and therefore the eponym for hermaphroditic animals.

Giant African land snails therefore have both female and male genital organs. When the snails mate, they first exchange their respective sperm, which is stored in the body. The mating act can even last several hours. The genitals, which are extended for mating and inserted into the partner, are located behind the head. Each snail then develops its eggs and fertilises them with the sperm of the other snail that has already been exchanged.

However, the development of the eggs often does not take place immediately after the mating act, but usually at a later time, when the snail decides that the conditions are now particularly good - because the sperm of the other snail can even be stored in the body for up to a year.

How long it then takes for the eggs to be laid varies from species to species. As a rule, the eggs are laid after a period of two to four weeks. For this purpose, the snail "digs" a kind of cave in the soil where the eggs are laid.

How many eggs are laid and how large these eggs are also varies greatly. Snails belonging to the Achatina genus lay very small eggs in a very large number. As a rule, the eggs are only about five millimetres in size. Sometimes the eggs reach a size of eight millimetres, which is still quite small. However, about three hundred eggs are laid in return.

The eggs of Archachatina snails are much larger - often about two centimetres in diameter - and therefore usually only about ten eggs are laid.

In addition, there are also a few giant African land snail species that are viviparous. So instead of eggs, small snail babies are already laid in the burrows. Examples of viviparous species are Achatina zanzibarica and Achatina iredalei.

If the giant African land snail lays eggs, it takes different lengths of time from species to species for small snail babies to hatch from the eggs. The large eggs of the genus Archachatina take quite a long time to hatch - usually after about one month to one and a half months. The small eggs of the Achatina snails usually hatch faster, in many cases after only two weeks.

If you keep several Achatina snails together, the hermaphroditism will inevitably cause the snails to mate sooner or later. However, this does not mean that hatching has to happen and that everyone should suddenly become a breeder. Breeding requires a lot of knowledge and experience. Since this is a book for beginners and since, in my opinion, beginners should not breed, the subject of breeding is not dealt with in this book. However, the question naturally arises as to what should happen to the laid eggs instead. I recommend freezing the eggs. Under no circumstances should the eggs be put directly into the rubbish because this way the cells are not yet killed. So before disposing of the eggs, it is a good idea to put them in the freezer for about two days.

© *Mrthoif0*

Purchasing the Snails

If one wants to acquire pets, many people almost automatically turn to a conventional pet shop. However, pet shops unfortunately often give the wrong advice, as the staff are often not specially trained in snails. This is not only the case with snails such as giant African land snails, but also with other popular pets such as reptiles, rodents, amphibians, fish, etc. Therefore, it is advisable to at least take the information from pet shops with a grain of salt.

Furthermore, pet shops often sell animals that are not ready to be given away - some animals are injured, some animals are ill, etc. It will usually be difficult for a layperson to judge whether an animal is ready to be surrendered.

It is therefore more advisable to buy giant African land snails from a reputable breeder. Reputable breeders concentrate either on a specific giant African land snail species or on a few different species. This allows them to gain a lot of experience and they are experts in their respective field. When they hand them over, the animals must be healthy, must not have any injuries and they must be old enough. It is not necessary that an giant African land snail is already fully grown when it is given away, but it must at least have reached its giving away age.

A reputable breeder will pay attention to all these points and give comprehensive advice to the new owner. Serious breeders attach great importance to their animals being placed in beautiful and species-appropriate homes and are therefore happy to answer any open questions.

Of course, it is also possible to take over giant African land snails from a care centre or second hand. Care centres are mostly privately owned and sometimes people come in need who unfortunately have to - or want to - give up their giant African land snails for a variety of reasons. Taking on giant African land snails second-hand because they are no longer wanted in their old home is also a laudable decision. However, there is a risk of unintentionally taking over sick animals that would be better off in expert hands until they are healthy again.

If there is no reputable breeder in the vicinity, animal transport or shipping is an option instead of collecting the animals in person. Professional animal transports pick up the animals and drive them to the new owner. However, whether animal shipping is allowed varies from country to country. Despite the greatest care, shipping always represents a stress factor and a risk. If possible, it is better to collect the animals in person or at least use professional animal transport.

© Barbara Konwischer

Single Keeping, Group, Socialisation?

Giant African land snails are not solitary animals, so they should not be kept alone. It is best to keep them at least in threes.

Sometimes keepers get the idea of housing different species, genera or even different snail families together. This is not advisable for several reasons.

Different species belonging to the same genus can usually mate with each other - and will do so sooner or later, as all giant African land snails are hermaphrodites. This gives rise to hybrids. This neither serves the conservation of the different species nor does it offer advantages for the snails.

Furthermore, snails sometimes have different requirements in terms of husbandry parameters. It is not always possible to provide optimal living conditions for every snail if the snails in a group do not belong to the same species. So, someone always has to "fall by the wayside". Especially the requirements for humidity and ambient temperature often differ; sometimes considerably, sometimes only minimally - but even with minimal differences, one species will have to lose out.

Although most (agate) snail species are peaceful, the different species can still interfere with each other. Often one species gains the upper hand because it is fitter and/or larger, and the other species has to be subordinate. Of course, especially predatory snail species should be avoided. With predatory species, the risk is very high that they will attack other snails.

Ethical aspects also play a role here. In the wild, different species of giant African land snails would not form a group - not only because this is often not possible due to spatial distance, but also because there is no reason to do so. A group with different snail species offers no advantages for the animals, but some risks. Therefore, it is always better to keep only snails of the same species together.

However, if you want to keep different species, this is of course no problem. Simply keep the different groups spatially separated from each other, for example in two different terrariums. These do not necessarily have to be in different rooms, but the different species should not have access to the other group.

Furthermore, the so-called "crowding effect" must be mentioned at this point. As the name already suggests, this is the problem of too many snails living together in an area that is too small. The population density in this area is too high and the snails cannot develop fully due to the lack of space.

In nature, the snails can regulate any overpopulation of the habitat themselves and expand the habitat, but this is of course not possible in the home terrarium, where the habitat is limited by humans. For this reason, the minimum dimensions should be observed in any case.

Although the crowding effect has so far only been proven for a few species (Lissachatina fulica, Limicolaria flammea, Lissachatina allisa), it is reasonable to assume that the other species also suffer from too high a population density.

In September 2000, for example, Sidel'nikov and Stepanov demonstrated the crowding effect in the Lissachatina fulica species from a population of ten snails per square metre (*Effect of the population density on growth and regeneration in the snail Achatina fulica*). The total volume is not taken into account here, because only the floor space (i.e., length x width of the terrarium) plays a role with regard to the crowding effect.

In the study mentioned above, it was also shown that the crowding effect can cause some serious health problems - of particular concern are reduced food consumption, reduced and poorer enclosure growth and, in the case of very high population density, even possible infertility or reduced fertility.

However, it does not matter whether the snails are still young or already fully grown. Young snails should also have enough space and not be kept in too small a space just because they are still small - because the crowding effect can also occur with them, and it is then all the more serious because the snails are still growing. Therefore, even young snails can already live in a large terrarium and do not have to be housed in boxes or similar beforehand.

Although snails should belong to the same species within a group and it is not recommended to socialise them with other species or even other snail families or species, socialisation with some specific "helpers" is quite reasonable. These include collembola, earthworms and isopods. These little animals help to keep the terrarium clean and contribute to a natural and species-appropriate habitat. For example, they take care of snail droppings and food remains. They can even help with possible mould.

It is well known that earthworms loosen the soil. In addition, they decompose organic matter such as food remains, which helps immensely with the general cleanliness of the snail home. Both red worms (Dendrobaena veneta, Eisenia hortensis) and dew worms (Lumbricus terrestris) are suitable.

If you want to put isopods in the snail home, the tropical white isopods (Trichorhina tomentosa) are particularly suitable. They reach a size of about three to four millimetres - so they remain very small. The tropical white isopods are also known as the "health police" or "environmental police" because they decompose organic substances or metabolic products (i.e., the faeces of the snails). If the tiny animals manage to escape the terrarium, however, there is no need to worry - because the tropical white isopods need high humidity and - as the name suggests - a tropical climate like in the terrarium to survive. So, in the home they would simply die. In the terrarium, however, they help maintain an ideal microclimate for the snails.

Springtails (=collembola) fulfil similar tasks. They are very good at preventing mould growth in the snail's home. Furthermore, collembolae are so-called "second decomposers"; this means that they decompose excrement, which is extremely helpful for cleanliness.

Worms, collembolae and isopods can also end up as live snail food, but this is perfectly fine and no cause for concern.

© *Inquiryml*

The Home of the Snails

We speak of the snails' "terrarium" in this book, but it must first be mentioned that terrariums are not the only possible homes for giant African land snails.

It is also possible to house giant African land snails in an aquarium or even in a very large box. However, it is not a good idea to keep the animals in the garden or similar, because in most countries - especially in Europe - there are no suitable environmental conditions for the African snails.

On the one hand, snails get used to their home, because they are loyal to their location. If they are taken away from their familiar environment, this means fear and stress for the animals. They also do not need fresh air or sunshine, because in their natural habitat the humidity is very high, and the air is therefore quite "stuffy". Especially after it has rained, giant African land snails feel very well, because this rain means a lot of moisture for them, which is essential. Therefore, giant African land snails do not crave direct sunlight, which can even dry them out.

On the other hand, the temperature fluctuations outside the house are usually too great and we have no influence on the respective weather. The climate in Africa cannot be compared with the climate in Europe, for example.

Furthermore, it should of course be avoided that the giant African land snails "run away" and suddenly multiply in the wild. Such cases have already occurred in the USA, the snails have multiplied rapidly in some cases and are now considered dangerous pests in the USA - also because cases of free-living giant African land snails carrying the rat lungworm have become known in the USA, as they must have come into contact with rat faeces in the wild. This has even led to giant African land snails no longer being legal in the USA. Of course, we would like to avoid such bans in other countries - especially because our dear giant African land snails in the terrarium at home are very harmless animals that do not cause any harm or transmit any diseases if they do not come into contact with the respective pathogens.

But now back to the terrariums, aquariums and boxes: In the vast majority of cases, snails are kept in a terrarium. However, aquariums and very large boxes can also be converted into a species-appropriate home for snails. In any case, it is important to ensure high humidity in the respective home at all times.

If you use a terrarium as a home for giant African land snails, the ventilation slits of the terrarium should be taped off as much as possible so that the humidity does not drop too much and the moist air cannot escape too much. However, it should be ensured that fresh oxygen can still enter the terrarium, so a few holes should remain. How many ventilation slits should be taped off varies from terrarium to terrarium - it is best to try out a little in which way the humidity remains nice and stable.

Traditionally, fish and other aquatic animals live in an aquarium. An aquarium is completely closed on all sides, so the stability of the high humidity is guaranteed here. However, it must be noted that fish, for example, take in their oxygen through the water in which they live - of course, giant African land snails do not do this. Therefore, the aquarium must not be completely closed so that fresh atmospheric oxygen can get in. If the aquarium has a lid with some air holes, this should be sufficient. Otherwise, the aquarium can also be closed with a plexiglass pane, for example, in which a few air holes have been drilled.

Boxes may also be suitable under certain circumstances, as long as they are large enough. The floor space must be guaranteed in any case. If this is the case, boxes are quite practical because they are light, because the humidity remains stable and because you can easily drill a few air holes into the hard plastic.

In any case, giant African land snails enjoy a large home and also need it to avoid being stressed and to avoid a crowding effect. Minimum home sizes vary from species to species as well as from country to country. Minimum sizes recommended in Germany may differ from minimum sizes recommended in the UK and so on. It is important to note here that this minimum size is set by humans and that snails in the wild naturally do not have such a limited habitat. So, if you have enough space, you should already give and allow the snails as much space as possible.

The crowding effect has so far only been proven for a few species, but it is therefore reasonable to assume that other species are also stressed by too high a population density and can develop health problems. The crowding effect has so far been proven for a number of ten snails per square metre. It does not matter whether the snails are still young or already fully grown - even young snails need sufficient space. One square metre of space (roughly ten square feet) for the giant African land snails is possible in most homes, even if the group consists of only three giant African land snails, for example. Nevertheless, it is good for the three snails to have a whole square metre of floor space at their disposal.

Examples of minimum sizes for different species (min. length x width x height):

Achatina achatina – 4 x 1.5 x 1.5 feet

Achatina craven – 2 x 1.5 x 1.5 feet

Archachatina marginata suturalis – 3 x 1.5 x 1.5 feet

Archachatina marginata ovum – 4 x 1.5 x 1.5 feet

Archachatina rhodostoma – 3 x 1.5 x 1.5 feet

Archachatina porphyrostoma – 2.5 x 1.5 x 1.5 feet

Archachatina knorii – 2.5 x 1.5 x 1.5 feet

Lissachatina fulica – 3 x 1.5 x 1.5 feet

Lissachatina iredalei sansibar – 3 x 1.5 x 1.5 feet

Lissachatina reticulata – 4 x 1.5 x 1.5 feet

Lissachatina immaculata – 3 x 1.5 x 1.5 feet

Lissachatina zanzibarica – 2.5 x 1.5 x 1.5 feet

Lissachatina allisa – 2.5 x 1.5 x 1.5 feet

The homes can always be even bigger!

Examples of appropriate humidity for different species:

Achatina achatina – 80 - 90%

Archachatina marginata suturalis – 90%

Archachatina marginata ovum – 90%

Archachatina rhodostoma – 90%

Archachatina knorii – 80 - 85%

Lissachatina fulica – 90%

Lissachatina iredalei sansibar – 90%

Lissachatina allisa – 80 - 90%

Examples of appropriate daytime temperatures for different species:

Achatina achatina – 26 - 28 °C

Archachatina marginata suturalis – 26 - 27,5 °C

Archachatina marginata ovum – 26 - 27,5 °C

Archachatina rhodostoma – 26 - 27,5 °C

Archachatina knorii – 26 - 27 °C

Lissachatina fulica – 26 - 27 °C

Lissachatina iredalei sansibar – 26 - 27 °C

Lissachatina allisa – 27 - 29 °C

At night, temperatures should be lowered by two to three degrees!

Now we want to look at what basic equipment the home for the giant African land snails should have ...

- ✓ suitable substrate (mainly soil)
- ✓ a heating mat for the right temperature or similar heating possibility

- ✓ some plants (the plants may need separate lighting)

- ✓ calcium (e.g., a bowl of cuttlefish)

- ✓ hygrometer to monitor humidity

- ✓ thermometer to monitor temperature

- ✓ natural material to keep the animals occupied (branches, roots, bark, etc.)

- ✓ foliage - dried leaves and/or fresh leaves

- ✓ retreat possibilities

- ✓ bathing bowl (shallow; snails cannot swim)

- ✓ water bowl

- ✓ optionally a food bowl, but this is not necessary - food can simply be distributed around the enclosure.

- ✓ helpers for the substrate (springtails, earthworms, tropical white isopods, etc.)

Normal, light organic potting soil is best suited as substrate. Snails like to burrow, so the substrate should be nice and loose and layered high enough.

The soil should be at least as high as the giant African land snails are tall - for example, if the snails in a group are about 15 centimetres tall, the substrate should also be about 15 centimetres high. An even higher substrate is of course also possible.

Doing without a substrate altogether is not an option. Nor should hard materials such as stone slabs or slate be used. Sand and gravel should also be avoided. Giant African land snails also do not need kitchen towels, toilet paper or similar as nesting material - for this they use the loose soil and gladly lots of dry and/or fresh leaves.

The light organic soil should be peat-free. In addition, it should be mixed with lime; conventional garden lime or similar lime is sufficient for this. The soil is mixed with the lime in a ratio of about 20:1 - so for every twenty litres of soil there is about 1 litre of lime.

Depending on the size of the enclosure and the size of the snails, this adds up to quite a lot of soil - it is not uncommon, for example, for 80 litres of soil to be needed to layer the entire home and reach the minimum height. But don't worry, as a rule the soil does not have to be replaced.

Little soil helpers such as earthworms, springtails and tropical white isopods create a natural habitat and even the faeces of the snails are utilised by the "environmental police". So, given an appropriate climate and good health, the little animals usually take care of keeping the home clean very independently.

Moreover, giant African land snails get used to their environment and a regular exchange of soil means stress for them. If the habitat is not too wet and there are no pests, changing the substrate is not necessary. However, every few months some new lime should be mixed into the soil.

We use a hygrometer to check the humidity in the snail home and a thermometer to check the temperature. There are also practical devices that measure and display both parameters simultaneously. But how do we achieve the right parameters in the first place?

If the humidity drops, you should have a normal spray bottle with water at hand. Spray the entire interior and the floor with this. The windows and walls can also be sprayed with water. However, you should refrain from spraying the water directly onto the snails themselves. We use a spray bottle so that the water is easily distributed everywhere, and everything is evenly moist - large puddles or water accumulations should be avoided. As a rule, you spray the home once a day.

To achieve the right temperature and keep it constant, heating mats are best suited. Many snail keepers also use spot heaters, which also serve to warm up the snails. However, it should be said that spot heaters are mainly used for reptiles - for example, geckos, bearded dragons and the like. These animals like to sunbathe and usually want to have three areas in their home: a hot area for sunbathing, a "normal" area and a cool area. Snails are not dependent on different heat zones and therefore do not really need spotlights. However, if spotlights are used to generate heat, this is perfectly fine. However, care should be taken to ensure that the snails are not burnt by spotlights that are too hot and that the heat is distributed reasonably evenly throughout the home.

A heating mat heats the snail home more evenly. It is attached to the outside of the terrarium (not the inside) and should be on the back wall or one of the side walls. It should not be attached underneath the home and should ideally not be level with the ground, as the giant African land snails bury themselves in the ground if they get too warm. They should be able to cool down in the soil.

The following formula has become established for calculating the required wattage of the heating mat:

Height x width x depth in decimetres x (target temperature - room temperature) ÷ 24 = wattage.

Example: The terrarium is 50 cm high, 100 cm wide and 50 cm deep. The temperature in the terrarium should be 27°C. The room temperature is 20°C.

Formula: 5 x 10 x 5 x (27-20) ÷ 24 = 73

The wattage of the heating mat should therefore be around 70-75 watts. This is only a rough guide to help you estimate the wattage needed.

For a natural and species-appropriate habitat, some plants are also important and should not be missing in any giant African land snail home. These also ensure a good climate and good air quality. Plants that cope well with the temperatures and humidity in the terrarium are particularly suitable.

Plants such as Ophiopogon, Bromeliads, Adiantum, Golliwoog, Acorus or Chlorophytum are quite popular. Depending on which plants you choose, they may need extra lighting. No separate lighting is necessary for the giant African land snails themselves.

© Onkel Ramirez

Diet and Nutrition

Animals are roughly divided into herbivores, carnivores and omnivores. Within these categories there are then further "specialisations". Insectivores, for example, belong to the carnivores and leaf-eaters to the herbivores.

Giant African land snails are omnivores - they can digest and use both plant and animal food. In nature, giant African land snails eat all kinds of plant food, but also help themselves to carrion, for example.

Many (not all!) giant African land snails prefer sweet food and disdain bitter plants. However, this also differs from snail to snail because tastes are different -

not only in humans, but also in giant African land snails. It is therefore a good idea to offer the giant African land snails a variety of different foods and to pay attention to what the snails particularly like.

Offering a variety of different foods is also important to provide the snails with a varied diet. Each food offers different macro- and micronutrients that help to supply the body with all essential nutrients. Of course, the snails do not need to be offered new plants every day, but there should always be a good selection available so that the snails can also select a little according to their needs.

Furthermore, animals are divided into "generalists" and "specialists". Generalist species can adapt quite well to their environment and use different resources, while specialist species use more limited food resources and are therefore more dependent on their environment as well as environmental conditions.

Generalist species such as giant African land snails can use a wide range of foods and are not particularly choosy, however many snails still have preferences for certain foods and sometimes an aversion to others.

The diet of giant African land snails should consist mainly of plant food. The focus should be on vegetables, fruit and (wild) herbs. In addition, giant African land snails may also eat seeds and nuts, as these contain healthy fats, for example, but due to their high energy density, seeds and nuts should only be fed sparingly and should be an occasional snack, for example.

On the other hand, you should avoid foods that are too spicy, such as onions. These are usually not touched by the snails anyway. Whether citrus fruits and cabbage varieties should be offered is very controversial in the snail community. It is often criticised that citrus fruits are too acidic and that cabbage causes flatulence. However, some snail keepers feed these foods without any problems if the snails have been slowly accustomed to them - but it is not necessary to feed them.

Furthermore, no cereals should be fed - feeding pasta, rice, bread and the like is neither necessary nor healthy. Dairy products should also be avoided, as milk and foods made from it, such as cheese, curd etc., are not part of a snail's species-appropriate diet.

Furthermore, snails must not eat salt or industrial sugar - naturally occurring fructose is of course perfectly fine.

Examples of well-suited vegetables (list not exhaustive):

- Broccoli

- Chicory

- Lamb's lettuce

- Fennel

- Cucumbers

- Kale

- Carrots

- Lettuce

- Sweet corn

- Pak choi

- Bell peppers (no hot chillies or similar)

- Parsnip

- Radicchio

- Rocket

- Spinach (not much, because of high oxalic acid content)

- Sweet potatoes

- Tomatoes (are actually a fruit)

- Courgette / Zucchini

Examples of well-suited fruits (list not exhaustive):

- Apples

- Apricots

- Bananas

- Pears

- Blackberries

- Strawberries

- Raspberries

- Honeydew melon

- Pumpkin

- Mangoes

- Passion fruit

- Nectarines

- Peach

- Grapes

Examples of well-suited herbs (list not exhaustive):

- Sorrel

- Basil

- Common plantain

- Nettles

- Daisies

- Goutweed

- Clover

- Cress

- Dandelion

- Parsley

- Yarrow

- Ribwort

Examples of well-suited tree leaves (list not exhaustive):

- Apple tree

- Beech tree

- Hornbeam

- Hazel

Many herbs such as dandelion, clover, ribwort plantain or goutweed can be wonderfully collected in the wild. However, it is advisable not to look for these herbs along busy roads or similar places, as they can be very polluted by exhaust fumes. Also, of course, one should not collect in places where pesticides, rat poisons or the like are used. As a rule, wild herbs are best found in public forests. Before feeding, the herbs - as well as the purchased food - should be washed well!

Furthermore, a sufficient supply of calcium is essential for giant African land snails. As we already know, the shell of the snails consists mostly of calcium

- about 98%. A sufficient supply of calcium through the normal diet is not always sufficient and covers the requirements. Therefore, giant African land snails are offered additional calcium, which they should be able to help themselves to freely. Calcium is not only particularly important for the snail shell, but also, for example, for the formation of the eggs, whose shell consists largely of calcium. In addition, young animals also have an increased need for calcium.

A large proportion of giant African land snail owners and giant African land snail breeders use cuttlefish powder (or ground cuttlefish shells) to ensure a sufficient supply of calcium. Sepia comes from the cuttlefish and in most cases smells correspondingly strong. Besides the important calcium, it also contains, for example, magnesium, zinc and iodine.

It must therefore be mentioned that not all snails like cuttlefish powder and consume it. Sometimes the grated cuttlebone is not offered in a small bowl but scattered directly in the terrarium. In pet shops it can often be found with the food for birds. If a snail does not accept the cuttlebone powder, there are many other odourless calcium powders on the market.

Calcium powders are divided into calcium citrate and calcium carbonate. Calcium citrate is artificially produced, whereas calcium carbonate is obtained from a naturally occurring source. Therefore, calcium carbonate usually has about four to five times the amount of calcium.

Sometimes the giant African land snails are also offered a lime food mash. In this case, the human mixes (usually different) food into a kind of mash and adds lime to this mash for the calcium supply. Personally, I advise against this, as the human determines how much or how little calcium the snail takes in. It is also not always clear whether the snail eats the lime food mash because it actually needs lime or because it is simply hungry. It is better to separate this and always offer the calcium in a separate bowl, which the snail can freely help itself to - far away from the "normal" food - because usually animals have a very good feeling for which micronutrients they need.

Nevertheless, the calcium should not be offered in a highly concentrated form (e.g., 100% calcium), but should be somewhat diluted. This is another reason why it is ideal to use cuttlebone as a calcium source, as the calcium has already been "stretched" in a natural way.

As we explained at the beginning of this chapter, snails are omnivorous animals. However, the proportion of animal food in the giant African land snail diet is minimal. It is sufficient to offer the giant African land snails only a little animal food about every fortnight. Dried or fresh insects are most suitable for this. Only small amounts should be fed, which will be eaten up by the giant African land snails within a short time, so that they do not remain in the enclosure.

Suitable foods include ...

... gammarus (brown shrimps)

... crickets

... mealworms

Furthermore, it has become established in many countries to regularly offer the giant African land snails some healing clay. Healing clay is not only good for supplementing the diet of sick or weakened snails, but also for disease prevention, to supply the body even better with essential minerals.

While calcium should always be freely available to the snails, healing clay is not usually offered in unlimited quantities. It is a good idea to sprinkle some healing clay into a small shallow bowl about once a week so that the snails can absorb some of it.

Lissachatina fulica shell. © Wolfgang Eckert

Diseases

Like all living creatures, giant African land snails can also fall ill. The prevention of diseases is always essential, because how often and how severely a creature falls ill can be determined to a large extent by humans. Animals that are kept in poor conditions and/or are not fed a healthy diet naturally fall ill more often and more severely than animals that have enough space, adequate humidity, healthy food, suitable temperatures, etc.

But sometimes luck - or rather bad luck - also plays a role. Even animals that live in perfect conditions can develop a more or less severe disease, which may or may not be due to genetics.

Since giant African land snails are nocturnal, diseases are often detected rather late. The first sign that an animal is not feeling well is almost always reduced food intake. If the giant African land snails (almost) only eat at night, it is sometimes not noticeable if a single snail has not helped itself to food and it has merely been eaten by the other snails. For this reason, too, you should try to keep an eye on whether all the snails are eating regularly. As snails have a fast metabolism and therefore lose weight very quickly if they do not eat or eat little, the diet is essential and should be observed regularly.

In addition to loss of appetite, lethargic behaviour is also a very common indication of disease. Giant African land snails are of course generally rather calm and slow-tempered, but if, for example, a snail hardly burrows any more and/or frequently retreats alone, this can be a sign of indisposition.

Dehydrated animals in particular need plenty of fluids. If a snail does not accept water, it is best to offer it cucumber slices, for example - cucumbers consist of about 97 percent water.

- Low humidity:

Too low humidity can be fatal for giant African land snails. It is not only important that the snails always consume enough liquid to avoid dehydration, but humidity from the outside is at least as important. If the humidity is too low, the shell and the body become too dry and the snail is forced to form a membrane at the openings of the shell to prevent its body from drying out further and to keep the dry air outside. In the worst case, the snail can become completely dehydrated and eventually die. If high humidity is quickly restored, the snail usually recovers quite quickly, but the animal should not be exposed to such a risk or stress.

- Calcium deficiency:

A calcium deficiency can be just as fatal for snails as insufficient humidity. Calcium is important for many animals - for example, also for reptiles and birds, as they also lay eggs for reproduction. Eggs consist for the most part of calcium and this is extracted from other parts of the animal's body in order to be able to form the eggs. Although there are a few giant African land snail species that are viviparous, the majority of species lay eggs. Even if no breeding is planned and the eggs are not to hatch but are removed from the terrarium, the snail still needs energy and nutrients to develop them. Since giant African land snails are not loners, but should and want to live in a group, and since they are also hermaphrodites, sooner or later egg laying will occur regularly. A second important reason why calcium is so important for giant African land snails is their shell. The snail shell also consists mainly of calcium. For a stable and well-formed shell, it is therefore important that the giant African land snail always has enough calcium available - after all, the shell houses and protects the visceral sac! The shell should always be handled with care so that no damage occurs, but in the case of minor damage (such as small cracks) the snail is even capable of repairing these on its own - provided it is supplied with sufficient calcium!

- Rat lungworm (Angiostrongylus cantonensis):

To begin with, the rat lungworm is a parasitic worm and by all means an extremely serious parasite that can cause great damage in the event of an infestation. It can even infect humans and is very dangerous as it can cause meningitis. Giant African land snails act as an intermediate host for the rat lungworm. However, it is a prejudice that many giant African land snails are carriers of this very worm. Usually, transmission occurs when a snail comes into contact with the faeces of a rat, for example when it eats the rat faeces. This may occur in the wild but is almost impossible if the snails are obtained from a reputable breeder or other reputable source. Furthermore, since giant African land snails should not be kept outdoors, such as in the garden, but in a species-appropriate terrarium with appropriate humidity and temperatures, it is almost impossible for pet giant African land snails to come into contact with rat droppings. Snails infested with this parasite have mainly been found in the wild in Asia, Australia, the Caribbean countries and the South Pacific region. In Europe, there were no or hardly any known cases. In the USA, infected snails have been found sporadically, for example in Mississippi and Louisiana. Unfortunately, this has given giant African land snails a bad reputation in many countries, which is hardly justified - because once again: if the snail comes from a reputable source and is kept at home under species-appropriate conditions, it does not come into contact with rats or their faeces at all.

- Penile prolapse:

Fortunately, penile prolapse is quite rare. The sexual act between two giant African land snails, i.e. mutual mating, is called copulation. For copulation, the sexual organs are extended and after completion, they retract again automatically - in most cases. Rarely, however, it happens that the snail is not able to retract the penis and it remains outside the body. This is very dangerous because the penis can dry out and will very likely die as a result. When the penis - or any other part of the body - dries out and dies due to lack of oxygen, this is called "necrosis"; so necrosis is dead tissue that can also inhibit or completely block all blood and nutrient supply in some circumstances.

Penile retraction can take some time and does not always happen immediately. However, if it is noticed that the penis is still hanging out a few hours after mating, you can try to help the snail in a gentle way, for example by dribbling some water on the penis or trying to push it back with very light pressure. However, this should always be done with a clean cotton bud or similar and it should not be pushed in forcibly as this could only cause more damage.

- Bacterial diseases:

As a rule, bacterial diseases in giant African land snails can in many cases be detected by skin lesions. A bacterial disease that occurs comparatively often in giant African land snails are aeromonads, which belong to the rod-shaped bacteria. Aeromonas is a genus of gram-negative gammaproteobacteria and usually causes skin diseases. The most common skin lesions are those in which the skin tissue tears and is destroyed - either all over the body or only in certain areas. The creeping foot or the antennae are frequently affected. In many cases, the top layer of skin (the epidermis) becomes lighter. Such a disease, like all diseases, should be taken seriously, but in most cases it is quite treatable with appropriate antibiotics.

- Rhabditids:

Rhabditids are parasites that are comparatively common in giant African land snails. They belong to the worms, more precisely to the nematodes, and are only a few millimetres in size.

Parasites are basically divided into ectoparasites and endoparasites. Ectoparasites are "external living" parasites, for example mites on the skin. Endoparasites are "inside-living" parasites.

Rhabditids are therefore classified as endoparasites.

Artificially created habitats - for example, in terrariums - cause an infestation to increase quite quickly if it is not recognised and treated at an early stage, because there is not too much space available in the terrarium. How strong or weak the parasite infestation is often also strongly depends on the animal's psyche. Stress, fear and other negative emotions weaken the animal's immune system and thus its defences.

Rhabditids should be taken extremely seriously, as they can have a significant impact on the health of the giant African land snail. The diseased snail usually has no or hardly any appetite, often loses weight rapidly and also often suffers from diarrhoea. Furthermore, this weakened condition can lead to apathy.

Dear reader: For independent authors, product reviews are the basis for the success of a book. Therefore, we depend on your reviews. This not only helps the authors, but of course also future readers and the animals. Therefore, I would be extremely grateful for a review on this book. Thank you very much.

I wish you all the best, much joy with your snails and the best of health!

Legal Notice

This book is protected by copyright. Reproduction by third parties is prohibited. Use or distribution by unauthorised third parties in any printed, audio-visual, audio or other media is prohibited. All rights remain solely with the author.

Author: Alina Daria Djavidrad

Contact: Wahlerstraße 1, 40472 Düsseldorf, Germany

© 2021 Alina Daria Djavidrad

1st edition (2021)

Room for Notes

Printed in Great Britain
by Amazon

19891838R00054